Learning to Love Me
Written by Karla Lewis, LPC-MHSP, NCC

© **Copyright 2020 by Karla Lewis**
All rights reserved. No parts or information from this book may be copied, written, or distributed without express and written permission from the author. All information included in this book is for educational purposes only. No material included takes the place of counseling from your mental health practitioner.

ISBN 978-1-1-79487-590-6

Dedication

This book is dedicated to my beautiful niece. I wish and pray for you all the best life has to offer.

Introduction

Hello! If you're reading this, you're about to begin a special journey! As a Licensed Professional Counselor and a woman who journals myself, I know that the practice of journaling can be both powerful and transformative. It is also an excellent way for people to get to know themselves better.

However, frequently when I ask clients to journal, they tell me that they don't know where to start or what to write. This clients' dilemma inspired me to do a prompt journal. I also noticed that many of my clients struggle with confidence or self-esteem, so I decided to make it a self-esteem journal that will help women get to know themselves more intimately.

My prayer is that this book will help women know their self-worth and operate more beautifully, powerfully, and authentically as themselves in the communities they live in.

Thank you for investing your time and resources in you! So many times we as women invest in everyone but ourselves but spending time journaling will afford you the opportunity to invest in someone very special-you!

You may want to keep your journal in a special, sacred place in your home or in your purse. If you keep it in your purse, you can jot down your thoughts, ideas, or affirmations in your spare time while you're on the go.

The place in which you decide to journal can be where you normally spend time in prayer; a prayer closet or altar. Designating a special place will also help you reverence and honor your journal time and increase the likelihood of you doing the exercises in it.

If you're new to journaling or it's been awhile since you've done some writing, please set aside a little time each day to do it. Start small. Dedicate around five to ten minutes at first and then gradually increase the amount you spend over time.

It's important that you be patient with yourself as you work through this book. Many feelings can surface and doing the exercises could cause you to be rawer emotionally than you normally are. It's imperative for you to be aware of this and engage in a lot of self-care during this time period.

Book a massage. Light scented candles. Watch your favorite movies or funny shows and take a nice, hot, long bath. Now is your time! Rid your space of any distractions. Get comfortable and let's get to work!

Acknowledgments

Special thanks to Dr. Marilyn Garrett and my family. I could not have completed this project without you!

This Space & Time Is Just For Me.

What is self-esteem?

It is how you see yourself and how you feel about you. It can also be your level of confidence in your abilities. Addressing an opportunity in this area of your life begins with awareness and identification of where your self-esteem is.

-Please rate your self-esteem on a scale of 1-10 with 1 being low and 10 being high. _____

If you rated yourself 1-3, you have very low self-esteem and you've got some important work to do.

If you rated yourself 4-6, you have low to moderate self-esteem and you could use some attention to this area in your life.

If you rated yourself 7-8, your self-esteem is at a good level but you could benefit from giving this some attention.

If you rated yourself 9-10, you have high self-esteem and you probably don't need to do much work in this area but it's possible that you may still need to get to know yourself on a deeper level. Doing the exercises in this journal can help you get there.

Now Is The Time For Self-Reflection & Assessment.

In this section, it's important for you to answer these questions honestly. Please write the first answers that come to mind. Your first answers are most likely your "true truths".

Who are you? To answer this question, you may need to reflect on your values and/or characteristics that are important to you. You may also want to ask trusted friends and family for their opinions of you.

_____
_____
_____
_____
_____
_____
_____
_____
_____
_____
_____
_____
_____
_____
_____
_____
_____
_____
_____
_____
_____
_____
_____

What's the first thing you think about in the morning? What's the first thing you do in the morning?

_____
_____
_____
_____
_____
_____
_____
_____
_____
_____
_____
_____
_____
_____
_____
_____
_____
_____
_____
_____
_____
_____

Who do you want to be? What is stopping you from getting there?

Healing My Hurts Takes Work.

What does loving you look like?

If you put you first more often, what would that look like?

_____
_____
_____
_____
_____
_____
_____
_____
_____
_____
_____
_____
_____
_____
_____
_____
_____
_____
_____

I'm Transforming From Wounded to Whole!

When did you notice a change or decrease in your self-esteem? Was there an event that triggered it?

_____
_____
_____
_____
_____
_____
_____
_____
_____
_____
_____
_____
_____
_____
_____
_____
_____
_____
_____
_____
_____
_____

What do you feel contributed to or caused your low/lower self-esteem?

Name someone whom you feel impacted your self-esteem in a negative way. What relation is that person to you? What happened?

_____
_____
_____
_____
_____
_____
_____
_____
_____
_____
_____
_____
_____
_____
_____
_____
_____
_____
_____
_____
_____

How could you have asserted yourself to change that narrative? What could you have done differently in that relationship to honor yourself more, if anything?

_____
_____
_____
_____
_____
_____
_____
_____
_____
_____
_____
_____
_____
_____
_____
_____
_____
_____
_____
_____
_____
_____

Let's Beast This!

What makes you feel down about yourself? Is it certain relationships or experiences you have?

What are some ways you can love yourself better? How do you show love to yourself now?

___

Witness It.

Allow It.

Release It.

Is there anything you don't like about yourself? Your appearance? Your personality or character?

_____
_____
_____
_____
_____
_____
_____
_____
_____
_____
_____
_____
_____
_____
_____
_____
_____
_____
_____
_____
_____
_____
_____
_____

Is there anything you need to forgive yourself for?
Guilt can lower self-esteem and create depression.

I Am Writing My Own Narrative.

What do you like about yourself? Your appearance? Your personality or character?

Please identify five negative thoughts or beliefs you have about yourself. Write down the first statements that come to mind. These thoughts can be formed from negative statements you heard growing up from family members, friends, or teachers. They can also be formed from any negative experiences you've had. You want to address and change these but first you need to identify them and write them here.

_____
_____
_____
_____
_____
_____
_____
_____
_____
_____
_____
_____
_____
_____
_____
_____
_____
_____
_____
_____
_____
_____
_____

Now please write five positive statements to counter those negative thoughts. For example, "I am beautiful!" Many times the positive sentiments will often be the opposite of the negative ones you have written down.

These positive statements are also known as affirmations. Affirmations and "I Am" statements are powerful because they "affirm" or "confirm" who we are or who we need to be or become. Many schools of thought and religious theologies teach that our thoughts are important and that they help shape our actions and habits and ultimately our future.

"Watch your thoughts, they become your words; watch your words, they become your actions; watch your actions, they become your habits; watch your habits, they become your character; watch your character, it becomes your destiny," Lao Tzu

Now, please spend time writing these affirmations several times; at least 3 times each in your journal daily.

_____
_____
_____
_____
_____
_____
_____
_____
_____
_____
_____
_____
_____
_____
_____

I Am Living A Life Of Purpose.

When you look in the mirror, what do you see?

I'm God's Girl!

Now it's time for you to do some "mirror work". Mirror work involves reciting these affirmations to yourself as you face a mirror. Say them with passion and conviction as you look yourself in the eyes. This may be difficult at first but it will get easier as you continue to practice it. You may have to give the convictions of your heart some time to catch up with the words you say from your mouth.

_____
_____
_____
_____
_____
_____
_____
_____
_____
_____
_____
_____
_____
_____
_____
_____
_____
_____
_____
_____
_____
_____
_____
_____
_____
_____

I'm Becoming The Best Version Of Me!

Now it will be important to practice thought redirection. It's important for you to "think about what you're thinking about". In other words, pay attention to the thoughts you have. When you notice a second or third time thinking a negative thought, stop and redirect yourself to a more positive thought.

The positive thought that you redirect yourself to can be one of your positive affirmations or a favorite memory or even a favorite joke. This is an integral part of you writing your own narrative. If you don't create your own narrative or concept of yourself, people will create it for you! You create it by feeding your spirit, heart, and mind with your own positive thoughts.

You can practice some thought redirection here.

_____
_____
_____
_____
_____
_____
_____
_____
_____
_____
_____
_____
_____
_____
_____
_____
_____
_____

What makes you feel worthy or important? Pay attention to whether your answer is internal, originating from within, or external, originating from without.

___

I Deserve This Time.

Are there some things you want to feel better about? How can you change them for the better?

I Will Enjoy This New Life I Create!

What steps do you take now to make sure you enjoy your life?

_____
_____
_____
_____
_____
_____
_____
_____
_____

What do you like to do for fun? What would you like to start doing that you haven't done before?

_____
_____
_____
_____
_____
_____
_____
_____
_____
_____
_____
_____

If I Walk With God I'm Never Alone.

What do you highly value about your life? What is most important to you?

_____
_____
_____
_____
_____
_____
_____
_____
_____
_____

How do you currently reward yourself for your accomplishments?

_____
_____
_____
_____

Please designate a list of rewards you want to give yourself for your next set of accomplishments.

_____
_____
_____
_____
_____

Dreams I Never Dared to Dream Are Coming True!

How often do you compare yourself to others? What do you say about yourself when you make these comparisons?

_____
_____
_____
_____
_____
_____
_____
_____

Who do you lean on for support? Who is your support team and why?

_____
_____
_____
_____
_____
_____
_____
_____
_____
_____
_____
_____
_____
_____

I Won't Give Up.

I Won't Back Down.

I Won't Give In.

I Will Win!

Who and what are some energy depleters in your life?

_____
_____
_____
_____
_____
_____
_____
_____
_____

How can you reduce or eliminate them?

_____
_____
_____
_____
_____
_____
_____
_____
_____

What positivity can you replace the depleters with?

_____
_____
_____
_____
_____
_____
_____
_____
_____

I'm Trusting God's Timing.

Are there any mental health issues you need to closely monitor such as depression, anxiety, bipolar disorder, or PTSD? _____

How are you handling self-care in this area?

_____
_____
_____
_____
_____
_____
_____
_____
_____

How do you practice your spirituality?

_____
_____
_____
_____
_____
_____
_____
_____
_____

How does your practice of spirituality impact your self-esteem? How would you like to change this?

_____
_____
_____
_____
_____

"I Am Fearfully and Wonderfully Made."

-Psalm 139:14

Coloring is therapeutic so I included a few coloring pages for you to enjoy and use as pause from your journaling. Use your favorite crayons, coloring pencils, or markers to fill in these calming scenes anyway you like.

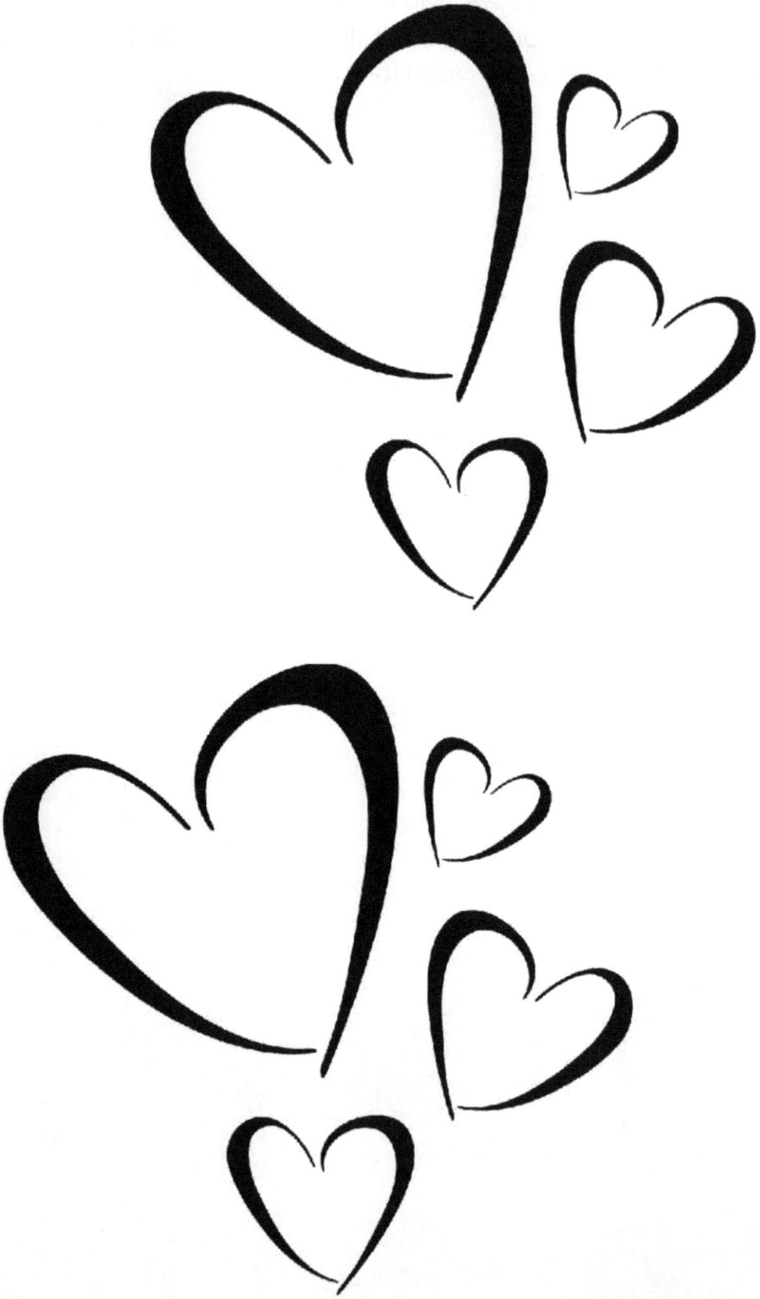

Prayer Gives Wings to God's Word!

Here is a list of songs I recommend you to listen to as you spend time journaling. These are just a few of my favorites and many of them are Contemporary Christian. You can also utilize instrumental music or soothing sounds found on some of today's popular music and meditation apps.

Torie Kelly- "Psalm 42"
Lady Gaga- "Heal Me"
India Arie- "He Heals Me"
Mary Mary-"I Survived"
Mandisa-"He Is With Me"
Seth and Nirva-"You Are With Me"
Zaneisha Davis' Album-"Crowned Affirmations"
Mariah Carey-"Hero"
Whitney and Mariah-"When You Believe"
Whitney Houston-"Greatest Love of All"
Aaliyah-"Journey to the Past"
Vernard Burton-"Finish Strong"
Joycylyn Wilson-"Something Beautiful"
Mary Mary-"Seattle"
Mary Mary-"Walking"
Christina Aguilera-"Reflection: This Girl I See"
Yanni Crawley-"The Promise"
Whitney Houston-"Didn't Know My Own Strength"
Yolanda Adams & Donnie McClurkin- "The Prayer"
Cece Winans-"I Surrender All"
Whitney & CeCe-"Count On Me"
Whitney Houston-"Shoop, Shoop"
Cece Winans-"I Am That I Am"
Tamela Mann-"Take Me to the King"
Tamela Mann-"I Can Only Imagine"
Donna Summer-"Forgive Me"
Cece Winans-"Alabaster Box"
Karla Michelle-"They Way That I Feel" & "Let Me Be An Instrument"
Kierra Sheard-"Indescribable"
Sherri Moffett-"Serenade"
Johnathan McReynolds-"Cycles"

I Owe it to Myself to Believe in Myself!

Thank you for your purchase and participation in this journal! Please let me know about your experience and thoughts with "Learning to Love Me: A Self-esteem Journal" at karlalewismotivates@gmail.com or www.coachkarla.com

Learning to Love Me

Learning to Love Me

Learning to Love Me

 *Learning to Love Me*

Learning to Love Me

Learning to Love Me

Learning to Love Me

Learning to Love Me

www.ingramcontent.com/pod-product-compliance
Lightning Source LLC
Chambersburg PA
CBHW032131090426
42743CB00007B/556